NOVEMBER 50 COLORING PAGES FOR ADULTS RELAXATION

SHIH CHIEN HUA

PUBLISHED BY:
SHIH CHIEN HUA
Copyright © 2018

SEABIRD SHOP >50FOR

FB FAN PAGE

Disclaimer

The information contained in this book is for general information purposes only. The information is provided by the authors and while we endeavor to keep the information up to date and correct, we make no representations or warranties of any kind, express or implied, about the completeness, accuracy, reliability, suitability or availability with respect to the book or the information, products, services, or related graphics contained in the book for any purpose. Any reliance you place on such information is therefore strictly at your own risk.

NOVEMBER 1ST

note:

_____

_____

_____

NOVEMBER 2ND

note:

_____

_____

_____

NOVEMBER 3RD

note:

_____

_____

_____

NOVEMBER 4TH

note:

_____

_____

_____

NOVEMBER 5TH

note:

_____

_____

_____

NOVEMBER 6TH

note:

_____

_____

_____

NOVEMBER 7TH

note:

_____

_____

_____

NOVEMBER 8TH

note:

_____

_____

_____

NOVEMBER 9TH

note:

_____

_____

_____

NOVEMBER 10TH

note:

_____

_____

_____

NOVEMBER 11TH

note:

_____

_____

_____

NOVEMBER 12TH

note:

_____

_____

_____

NOVEMBER 13TH

note:

_____

_____

_____

NOVEMBER 14TH

note:

_____

_____

_____

NOVEMBER 15TH

note:

_____

_____

_____

NOVEMBER 16TH

note:

_____

_____

_____

NOVEMBER 17TH

note:

_____

_____

_____

NOVEMBER 18TH

note:

_____

_____

_____

NOVEMBER 19TH

note:

_____

_____

_____

NOVEMBER 20TH

note:

_____

_____

_____

NOVEMBER 21TH

note:

_____

_____

_____

NOVEMBER 22TH

note:

_____

_____

_____

NOVEMBER 23TH

note:

_____

_____

_____

NOVEMBER 24TH

note:

_____

_____

_____

NOVEMBER 25TH

note:

_____

_____

_____

NOVEMBER 26TH

note:

_____

_____

_____

NOVEMBER 27TH

note:

_____

_____

_____

NOVEMBER 28TH

note:

_____

_____

_____

NOVEMBER 29TH

note:

_____

_____

_____

NOVEMBER 30TH

note:

_____

_____

_____

NOVEMBER 31TH

note:

_____

_____

_____

NOVEMBER 32TH

note:

_____

_____

_____

NOVEMBER 33TH

note:

_____

_____

_____

NOVEMBER 34TH

note:

_____

_____

_____

NOVEMBER 35TH

note:

_____

_____

_____

NOVEMBER 36TH

note:

_____

_____

_____

NOVEMBER 37TH

note:

_____

_____

_____

NOVEMBER 38TH

note:

_____

_____

_____

NOVEMBER 39TH

note:

_____

_____

_____

NOVEMBER 40TH

note:

_____

_____

_____

NOVEMBER 41TH

note:

_____

_____

_____

NOVEMBER 42TH

note:

_____

_____

_____

NOVEMBER 43TH

note:

_____

_____

_____

NOVEMBER 44TH

note:

_____

_____

_____

NOVEMBER 45TH

note:

_____

_____

_____

NOVEMBER 46TH

note:

_____

_____

_____

NOVEMBER 47TH

note:

_____

_____

_____

NOVEMBER 48TH

note:

_____

_____

_____

NOVEMBER 49TH

note:

_____

_____

_____

NOVEMBER 50TH

note:

_____

_____

_____

www.ingramcontent.com/pod-product-compliance
Lightning Source LLC
Chambersburg PA
CBHW081606220526
45468CB00010B/2790